NEW

AND

SELECTED

POEMS

NEW

AND

SELECTED

POEMS

Marie Howe

W. W. NORTON & COMPANY

Independent Publishers Since 1923

Manufacturing by Versa Press
Book design by Chris Welch
Production manager: Lauren Abbate

ISBN: 978-1-324-07503-5

W. W. Norton & Company, Inc.
500 Fifth Avenue, New York, N.Y. 10110
www.wwnorton.com

W. W. Norton & Company Ltd.
15 Carlisle Street, London W1D 3BS

1 2 3 4 5 6 7 8 9 0

For Grace Yi-Nan Howe

CONTENTS

New Poems (2023)

From *The Good Thief* (1987)

From *What the Living Do* (1997)

From *The Kingdom of Ordinary Time* (2008)

From *Magdalene* (2017)

New Poems

Prologue

In the middle of my life—just past the middle—

walking along the street with our little dog Jack on a leash

—Ok—just past the late-middle—

in what some might call early old age,

on a street crowded with children and tourists

my father dead, my mother dead,

my young husband gone from me and grown older (a father,

a husband now to someone else),

Jason dead, John dead, Jane and Stanley and Lucy and Lucie

and Billy and Tony and now Richard dead,

I came to the edge

and I did not know the way.

Postscript

What we did to the earth, we did to our daughters

one after the other.

What we did to the trees, we did to our elders

stacked in their wheelchairs by the lunchroom door.

What we did to our daughters, we did to our sons

calling out for their mothers.

What we did to the trees, what we did to the earth

we did to our sons, to our daughters.

What we did to the cow, to the pig, to the lamb,

we did to the earth, butchered and milked it.

Few of us knew what the bird calls meant

or what the fires were saying.

We took of earth and took and took, and the earth

seemed not to mind,

until one of our daughters shouted: *It was right*

in front of you, right in front of your eyes

and you didn't see,

The air turned red.   The ocean grew teeth.

Practicing

Today I'm going to practice being dead for a few hours.

No one can expect anything from me.

No emails. No groceries.

Our little dog Jack watches me walk

from room to room, but,

for a few hours, he is the only one who can,

and he returns contentedly to his bone.

I say bone—it's what the pet store calls

a bully stick, which is in fact a bull's penis—

dried out and hard.

That a small dog should chew on a bull's penis!

Well, we eat swordfish, don't we?

And the shy octopus whose brains

are in her arms?

The sunlight enters the small kitchen

spilling across the white enamel table

and the chipped blue wooden chair

whether anyone is there to see it, or not.

Meister Eckhart says, *There never was a man who forsook himself so much*

that he could not still find more in himself to forsake.

Nevertheless, it's good to have a dog with you when you are practicing

not being there: you don't feel so all alone.

The Saw, The Drill

There's always a chain saw somewhere,

the high whine of a drill, somebody building something or

tearing it down—fastening metal to metal.

When did wood give way to iron?

Then to plastic?

Almost everywhere the sound of the human will:

the bluster of engine, the grind of a blade, the wheel:

hammering, construction, repair.

Someone nailed to a cross, someone leashed, lashed.

Someone hung from a scaffold: listen: the squeak of the rope

the hammering.

Kill him with his own gun, a woman shouted,

Kill him with his own gun.

What have we made? What are we making?

And who or what made us that we should make

such things as we do and did?   We grow smaller.   We break things.

Then turn to each other and beg for what no human can give.

Reincarnation

Sometimes when I look at our dog Jack I think

he might be my radical American History professor come back

to make amends—he gazes at me so sorrowfully.

What is it Jack, I say, why do you look like that? But Jack

doesn't answer; he lies down and rests his head on his paws.

Black hair covered nearly all of that man's body, thick

under his blue oxford shirt when I put my hand there.

Perhaps that accounted for the bow tie,

the pipe, the tweed cap.

This time I can teach him to sit and to stay.

Stay, I say to Jack who looks at the treat in my hand

and then at me, and at the treat and then at me, and he stays.

Come, I say to Jack, but Jack does not always come.

Sometimes he sits and looks at me a long time,

as when my professor would lean back in his chair

draw on his pipe and gaze at me.

But when I hold a treat Jack comes, and I remember how

the professor would lick dripping honey from the jar

lick peanut butter from the knife.

A little stubborn, our dog Jack,

shy we thought,

until the morning my daughter jumped on my bed

and Jack sprang at her growling,

and the next morning when he rushed towards her growling

and bit her skirt and tore it, and bit her and broke her skin,

and when I went to collar him, bit me, snarling and bit and bit.

That's when I was pretty sure he was my history professor.

The vet said this happens more often than you'd imagine.

He must always be tethered, she said, until he can be trusted.

He must learn that you and your daughter come first.

And no more couch and no more sleeping in the bed with you Mama,

not ever.

I finally left him so late at night it was nearly dawn—

picking up my boots by the door,

stepping down the two flights, then running towards the car.

What can I say?   Jack may be my American History professor come back,

After all these years to make amends,

or Jack may be actually himself—a dog.

Another Theory of Time

So, I tell my daughter

—we are eating dinner, reading through the book of stories—

I'm worried about Jason. If I seem distracted, that's what's on my mind.

And she says, Take it out of your mind,

then dips and eats a dumpling, and says, But don't take out Jason.

And this morning at the deli I say, I'm grumpy because

it's the first day of school, and I'm thinking of so many things.

and she says, Take them out, and I say, How do I do that?

and she says, Think about Now.

I bite into my egg and cheese on a sesame bagel, and it is good. It is.

Although it does bother me—

how she always wants to sit at the tiny deli counter

so near the garbage bins—eating meatballs for breakfast.

Then she says, I can't remember the future *or* the past.

The local high school girls order iced coffee and whole wheat bagels

with nothing on them.   My girl eats her meatballs,

and I stare past the cutouts of ham and turkey taped to the window

and think about the moment I want so much to leave

—how small it is sometimes, this Now—

how constricting, me with my bad teeth and aging elbows,

as person after person tosses their trash inches behind my back

before walking out the open door.

Persephone

People forget he was a king, a god,

and that down there deep

everything gleamed.

So tight did he hold me I was swaddled hard

so bound I couldn't move,

and inside that grip he moved   and moved

                        and it was a monstrosity

an ecstasy.   I forgot myself.   I became

an animal again   I screamed.   It didn't matter how long.

No one put a hand over my mouth.

                And when it was over

I lay across his knees, on my back, entirely open,

nobody, no one

an animal on the altar of a king—a god.

Persephone, in the meadow

When I looked at the meadow flowers,

many of them looked back

offering their faces: sometimes crawling with ants or a bee.

And that was that.

But after I'd spent several hours with my mother

I often felt her face on my face—as if my face *were* her face.

After leaving my mother I'd go to the mirror and look and look

And it was my face I saw.

But from the inside it felt like hers,

and it was hours before I felt her likeness fade.

Persephone and Demeter

My mother needn't have pretended to be appalled,

she knows all about the under dark.

The seed must break open to rise.

My mother is a god; she wanted to spare me.

But my nature *is* nature.

Like everything alive   I was meant to be split open,

to blossom, to be sucked, to be eaten,

to lean, to bend, to wither,

to die and die and die until I died.

Advent

Not that we knew or could imagine

what some mild blue evenings made us homesick for.

Call it forethought but not thought of,

not conceived exactly.

When it happened, we said we saw it coming

approaching a horizon we hadn't

known was there. It occurred to us

at once—which altered time thereafter.

By then we could not remember the before

before it had the after in it.

What the Earth Seemed to Say, 2020

Do you still believe in borders?

Birds soar over your maps and walls, and always have.

You might have watched how the smoke from your own fires

travelled on wind you couldn't see

                        wafting over the valley

and up and over the hills and over the next valley and the next hill

Did you not hear the animals howl and sing?

Or hear the silence of the animals no longer howling?

Now you know what it is to be afraid.

You think this is a dream? It is not

a dream.   You think this is a theoretical question?

What do you love more than what you imagine is your singular life?

The water grows clearer. The swans settle and float there.

Are you willing to take your place in the forest again?

To become loam and bark, to be a leaf falling from a great height,

to be the worm who eats the leaf,

and the bird who eats the worm?   Look at the sky—are you

willing to be the sky again?

You think this lesson is too hard for you.

You want the time-out to end. You want

to go to the movies as before, to sit and eat with your friends.

It can end now, but not in the way you imagine.   You know

the mind that has been talking to you for so long, the mind that

can explain everything?   Don't listen.

You were once a citizen of the country called: *I Don't Know.*

Remember the boat that brought you there? It was your body. Climb in.

The Letter, 1968

That he wrote it with his hand and folded the paper

and slipped it into the envelope and sealed it with his tongue

and pressed it closed so I might open it with my fingers.

That he brought it to the box and slipped it through the slot

so that it might be carried through time and weather to where

I waited on the front porch step.

        (We knew how to wait then—it was what life was,

much of it.) So, when the mailman came up the walk and didn't have it

he might have it the next day or the next when it bore the mark

of his hand who had written my name, so I might open it and read

and read it again, and then again, and look at the envelope he'd sealed

and press my mouth to where his mouth had been.

The Forest

A mast year for acorns, so like marbles and so many

we're afraid of falling.   I walk sideways

down the hill, holding a long stick; Kate goes before me

wearing her orange knit cap.

The broken trees lean on the unbroken trees

which will one day be broken.

The Maples

I asked the stand of maples behind the house,

How should I live my life?

They said, shhh shhh shhh . . .

How should I live, I asked, and the leaves seemed to ripple and gleam.

A bird called from a branch in its own tongue,

And from a branch, across the yard, another bird answered.

A squirrel scrambled up a trunk

then along the length of a branch.

Stand still, I thought,

See how long you can bear that.

Try to stand still, if only for a few moments,

drinking light   breathing.

Jack and the Moon

After driving home through the forest,

I curled into bed to sleep, but Jack wouldn't let me.

He whined and barked—high-pitched barks I'd not heard before.

No, I said, from under the blanket. No.

Still, he barked and paced and paced and barked, No Jack!

Then yelped strange high yelps, followed by low growls, as if he might,

by the mere scope and scale of his pleading, persuade me,

until I did finally throw off the covers and open the front door

through which he hurried, not to sniff or pee, but to sit on the lawn,

his back to me, a small white dog facing the moon

lit by light so bright I could have read these words within it.

And when I went to fetch him, he scooted farther away to sit

tucked into himself, gazing into the flooded distance.

A very cold night—I stood a while at the open door—calling Jack!

Jack come, come now! (willful, stubborn dog!)

And when he didn't come, I curled up on the couch,

wrapped in a shawl and dozed for I don't know how long . . .

then woke, went again to the door and said quietly, Jack.

It was then he turned and came in, cold and calm, soaked with the moon.

Before

The boulder once dust, will be dust again,

but today, so filled with its own heaviness,

it can't hear the grunts of the men who push and roll it

to the mouth of the tomb,

and it can't yet conceive how else it might be moved.

Seventy

So, I've grown less apparent apparently:

The young men walk their dogs, and when our dogs meet

we look at the dogs without raising our eyes to each other.

The fathers stand outside the elementary school laughing

with the mothers—*Exactly*, one of them says to the other—

my passing presence faded like a well-washed once-blue cotton shirt.

Finally, I can slip through the world without being so adamantly in it.

And look, here comes the blind photographer

walking, as he does, his hand resting on the shoulder of his companion.

And now the riot of children pouring through the open school doors.

Late winter, an unseasonably warm afternoon

and the summer ice cream truck at the corner—

cold early March and there it is—playing its familiar kooky tune.

The Willows

As we are made by what moves us,

willows pull the water up into their farthest reach

which curves again down

divining where their life begins.

So, under travels up, and down and up again,

and the wind makes music of what water was.

Hymn

It began as an almost inaudible hum,

      low and long for the solar winds

          and far dim galaxies,

a hymn growing louder, for the moon and the sun,

      a song without words for the snow falling,

          for snow conceiving snow

conceiving rain, the rivers rushing without shame,

      the hum turning again higher—into a riff of ridges

          peaks hard as consonants,

summits and praise for the rocky faults and crust and crevices

      then down down to the roots and rocks and burrows

          the lakes' skittery surfaces, wells, oceans, breaking

waves, the salt-deep: the warm bodies moving within it:

      the cold deep: the deep underneath gleaming, some of us rising

          as the planet turned into dawn, some lying down

as it turned into dark; as each of us rested—another woke, standing

among the cast-off cartons and automobiles;

we left the factories and stood in the parking lots,

left the subways and stood on sidewalks, in the bright offices,

in the cluttered yards, in the farmed fields,

in the mud of the shanty towns, breaking into

harmonies we'd not known possible. finding the chords as we

found our true place singing in a million

million keys the human hymn of praise for every

something else there is and ever was and will be:

the song growing louder and rising.

(Listen, I too believed it was a dream.)

The Singularity

(after Stephen Hawking)

Do you sometimes want to wake up to the singularity

we once were

so compact nobody

needed a bed, or food or money

nobody hiding in the school bathroom

or home alone

pulling open the drawer

where the pills are kept.

For every atom belonging to me as good

belongs to you.   Remember?

There was no *Nature.*   No

them.   No tests

to determine if the elephant

grieves her calf   or if

the coral reef feels pain.   Trashed

oceans don't speak English or Farsi or French;

would that we could wake up to what we were

when we *were* ocean,   and before that

to when sky was earth, and animal was energy, and rock was

liquid, and stars were space, and space was not

at all—nothing,

before we came to believe humans were so important

before this awful loneliness.

Can molecules recall it?

What once was?   Before anything happened?

No I, no we, no one, no was

no verb   no noun

only a tiny tiny dot brimming with

is is is is is

All   everything   home.

The Good Thief

■

The danger itself fosters the rescuing power

—HÖLDERLIN

Part of Eve's Discussion

It was like the moment when a bird decides not to eat from your hand,
and flies, just before it flies, the moment the rivers seem to still
and stop because a storm is coming, but there is no storm, as when
a hundred starlings lift and bank together before they wheel and drop,
very much like the moment, driving on bad ice, when it occurs to you
your car could spin, just before it slowly begins to spin, like
the moment just before you forgot what it was you were about to say,
it was like that, and after that, it was still like that, only
all the time.

Death, the Last Visit

Hearing a low growl in your throat, you'll know that it's started.
It has nothing to ask you. It only has something to say, and
It will speak in your own tongue.

Locking its arm around you, it will hold you as long as you ever wanted.
Only this time it will be long enough. It will not let go.
Burying your face in its dark shoulder, you'll smell mud and hair and water.

You'll taste your mother's sour nipple, your favorite salty cock
and swallow a word you thought you'd spit out once and be done with.
Through half-closed eyes you'll see that its shadow looks like yours,

a perfect fit. You could weep with gratefulness. It will take you
as you like it best, hard and fast as a slap across the face,
or so sweet and slow you'll scream give it to me until it does.

Nothing will ever reach this deep. Nothing will ever clench this hard.
At last (the little girls are clapping, shouting) someone has pulled
the drawstring of your gym bag closed enough and tight. At last

someone has knotted the lace of your shoe so it won't ever come undone.
Even as you turn into it, even as you begin to feel yourself stop,
you'll whistle with amazement between your residual teeth oh jesus

oh sweetheart, oh holy mother, nothing nothing nothing ever felt this good.

What the Angels Left

At first, the kitchen scissors seemed perfectly harmless.
They lay on the kitchen table in the blue light.

Then I began to notice them all over the house,
at night in the pantry, or filling up bowls in the cellar

where there should have been apples. They appeared under rugs,
lumpy places where one would usually settle before the fire,

or suddenly shining in the sink at the bottom of soupy water.
Once, I found a pair in the garden, stuck in turned dirt

among the new bulbs, and one night, under my pillow,
I felt something like a cool long tooth and pulled them out

to lie next to me in the dark. Soon after that I began
to collect them, filling boxes, old shopping bags,

every suitcase I owned. I grew slightly uncomfortable
when company came. What if someone noticed them

when looking for forks or replacing dried dishes? I longed
to throw them out, but how could I get rid of something

that felt oddly like grace? It occurred to me finally
that I was meant to use them, and I resisted a growing compulsion

to cut my hair, although, in moments of great distraction,
I thought it was my eyes they wanted, or my soft belly

—exhausted, in winter, I laid them out on the lawn.
The snow fell quite as usual, without any apparent hesitation

or discomfort. In spring, as I expected, they were gone.
In their place, a slight metallic smell, and the dear muddy earth.

The Meadow

As we walk into words that have waited for us to enter them, so
the meadow, muddy with dreams, is gathering itself together

and trying, with difficulty, to remember how to make wildflowers.
Imperceptibly heaving with old impatience, it knows

for certain that two horses walk upon it, weary of hay.
The horses, sway-backed and self-important, cannot divine

how the small white pony mysteriously escapes the fence every day.
This is the miracle just beyond their heavy-headed grasp,

and they turn from his nuzzling with irritation. Everything
is crying out. Two crows, rising from the hill, fight

and caw-cry in mid-flight, then fall and light on the meadow grass
bewildered by their weight. A dozen wasps drone, tiny prop planes,

sputtering into a field the farmer has not yet plowed,
and what I thought was a phone, turned down and ringing,

is the knock of a woodpecker for food or warning, I can't say.
I want to add my cry to those who speak for the sound alone.

But in this world, where something is always listening, even
murmuring has meaning, as in the next room you moan

in your sleep, turning into late morning. My love, this might be
all we know of forgiveness, this small time when you can forget

what you are. There will come a day when the meadow will think
suddenly, *water, root, blossom,* through no fault of its own,

and the horses will lie down in daisies and clover. Bedeviled,
human, your plight, in waking, is to choose from the words

that even now sleep on your tongue, and to know that tangled
among them and terribly new is the sentence that could change your life.

The Split

I.

She'd start the fires under the bed.
I'd put them out.

She'd take the broom stick and rape all the little girls.
I'd pull them aside, stroke their cheeks, and comfort them.
—How they would cry.

Brit would fight the German soldiers.
She'd crouch by the banister waiting for them
when I was too scared.

And sometimes, she would push me farther into the back woods
than I wanted to go
But I was glad she did.

She was mean and she liked it.

She'd take off her clothes and dance in front of the mirror
and she'd say things and she'd swear.

She'd laugh at the crucifix, turn him upside down and watch him hang.
And she'd unhinge that piece of metal cloth between his legs
and run when she heard somebody coming
leaving me.

Mean as she was, I miss her.

Only twice have I heard her laugh since then.
Once, lying on my back in a yellow field,
I heard something that sounded like me in the back of my head
but it was Brit,

and just now, making love with you, it's hard to tell you
but I heard her laugh.

II.

It began as a fear.
There was something, not me, in the room.

And translated into a dumbfounding
forgetfulness

that stopped me on the street
puzzling

over what year it was, what month.

I began to watch my feet carefully.
Nevertheless, I suffered
accidents.

The bread knife sliced my thumb
repeatedly

the water glass shattered on the kitchen floor
and in its breaking there was a low laugh.

Looking up, I saw no one

but felt the old cat stretch inside me
feigning indifference.

Marie, I'd hear in a crowd, *Marie*
the air so thick with ghosts it was hard
breathing.

One afternoon, the trucks were humming like vacuum cleaners
in the rain.

It was impossibly lonely,
No one but me there:

I called out Brit, the city is burning,
Brit, the soldiers are coming

and she laughed so sudden and loud I turned
and saw her for one second

all insolent grace, pretending
she wasn't loving me.

What Belongs to Us

Not the memorized phone numbers.

The carefully rehearsed short cuts home.

Not the summer, shimmering like pavement, when Lucia
pushed Billy off the rabbit house and broke his arm,

or our tiny footprints in the back files.

Not the list of kings from Charlemagne to Henry

not the boxes under our beds

or Tommy's wedding day when it was so hot and Mark played the flute
and we waved at him waving from the small round window in the loft,

the great gangs of people stepping one by one into the cold water.

I have, of course, a photograph:
you and I getting up from a couch.

Full height, I stand almost two inches taller than you
but the photograph doesn't show that,
just the two of us in motion
not looking at each other, smiling.

Not even the way we said things, leaning against the kitchen counter.

Not the cabin where I burned my arm and you said, oh, you're the type
that if it hurt, you wouldn't say.

Not even the blisters. Look.

Gretel, from a sudden clearing

No way back then, you remember, we decided,
but forward, deep into a wood

so darkly green, so deafening with birdsong
I stopped my ears.

And that high chime at night,
was it really the stars, or some music

running inside our heads like a dream?
I think we must have been very tired.

I think it must have been a bad broken-off
piece at the start that left us so hungry

we turned back to a path that was gone,
and lost each other, looking.

I called your name over and over again,
and still you did not come.

At night, I was afraid of the black dogs
and often I dreamed you next to me,

but even then, you were always turning
down the thick corridor of trees.

In daylight, every tree became you.
And pretending, I kissed my way through

the forest, until I stopped pretending
and stumbled, finally, here.

Here too, there are step-parents, and bread
rising, and so many other people

you may not find me at first. They speak
your name, when I speak it.

But I remember you before you became
a story. Sometimes, I feel a thorn in my foot

when there is no thorn. They tell me,
not unkindly, that I should imagine nothing here.

But I believe you are still alive.
I want to tell you about the size of the witch

and how beautiful she is. I want to tell you
the kitchen knives only look friendly,

they have a life of their own,
and that you shouldn't be sorry,

not for the bread we ate and thought
we wasted, not for turning back alone,

and that I remember how our shadows walked
always before us, and how that was a clue,

and how there are other clues
that seem like a dream but are not,

and that every day, I am less
and less afraid.

Keeping Still

If late at night, when watching the moon, you still
sometimes get vertigo, it's understandable
that you wish suddenly and hard for fences, for someone
to marry you. Desiring a working knowledge,
needing to know some context by heart, you might
accept anything: the room without windows,
the far and frozen North, or the prairie, the prairie
even, if it means that.

The long wide space and cold dirt that will not
be seduced into hills, and the dust, that even after
you have kicked and wept and fallen on it pounding,
will not produce a tree. It will allow you
to rise with certainty and move with the relief
of necessary things to the wash on the line,
to the small maple you brought here that must be tied
for the winter or die.

Even the prairie night, blind with snow,
when no one comes, and you no longer look
to the mirror but force your fingers to the stitching
and produce a child to help with the lambing
and the carrying of water. Although it might be years
before you turn and stop, startled
by the sweet and sudden smell of sheets snapping
in the sun, and the drunken lilac, prairie purple,
blooming by the doorway, because you planted it.

Without Devotion

Cut loose, without devotion, a man becomes a comic.
His antics are passed

around the family table and mimicked so well, years
later the family still laughs.

Without devotion, any life becomes a stranger's story
told and told again to help another sleep

or live. And it is possible
in the murmuring din of that collective loyalty

for the body to forget what it once loved.
A mouth on the mouth becomes a story mouth.

It's what they think *they* knew—what the body knew
alone, better than it ever knew anything.

Without devotion, his every gesture—
how he slouched in the family pantry, his fingers

curled into a fist, the small things he said
while waiting for water to boil—

becomes potentially hilarious. Lucky for him
the body, sometimes, refuses translation,

that often it will speak, secretly,
in its own voice, and insist, haplessly,

on its acquired tastes. Without devotion, it might
stand among them and listen, laughing,

but look, how the body clenches,
as the much discussed smoke intermittently clears.

It has remembered the man standing, wearing
his winter coat.

Watch how it tears from the table, yapping, ferocious
in its stupid inarticulate joy.

Sorrow

So now it has our complete attention, and we are made whole.
We take it into our hands like a rope, grateful and tethered,
freed from waiting for it to happen. It is here, precisely
as we imagined.

If the man has died, if the child's illness has taken a sudden
turn, if the house has burned in the middle of the night
and in winter, there is at least a kind of stopping that will
pass for peace.

Now when we speak it is with great seriousness, and when
we touch it is with our own fingers, and when we listen
it is with our big eyes that have looked at a thing
and have not blinked.

There is no longer any reason to distrust us. When it leaves
it will leave like summer, and we will remember it as a break
in something that had seemed as unrelenting as coming rain
and we will be sorry to see it go.

Mary's Argument

"Let what you have said be done to me" *(Luke 1:38)*

To lead the uncommon life is not so bad.
There is an edge we come to count on
when all the normal signs don't speak,
a startled vigilance that keeps us waking
to watch the moon, the peculiar stars;
the usual, underfoot, no more a solid comfort
than a rock that might move as a turtle moves,
so slowly only the nervous feel the sudden bump
of the familiar giving way to unrequested astonishment.
As for a small time, the sheer cliff of everything
we never knew can rise in front of us
like the warm dark, where starlight
has its constant conception, where the *idea* of turtle
blinked and was: a wry joke, an intricate affection.

Encounter

First, the little cuts, then the bigger ones,
the biggest, the burns. This is what God did
when he wanted to love you.

She didn't expect to meet him on the stairway
no one used but she did, because she was
afraid of the elevator, the locked room.

She didn't expect him to look like that, to be
so patient, first the little ones, then
the big ones. Everything

in due time, he said, I've got all the time
in the world. She didn't imagine it would take
so long, the breaking.

He did it three times before he did it. Love?
She had imagined it differently, something
coming home to her,

an end to waiting. And she did stop, when
the big cuts came. It was all there was,
the burning, and that's what God was

everywhere at once. Someone had already
told her that, not only in his voice. He was
inside her now—

the bigger ones, then the burning—and gone,
then back again. This was eternity, when
nothing happened that wasn't

already happening. She couldn't remember.
After the burning, even the light went quiet.
She didn't think God would be so

specific, so delicate—inside her elbow, under
her arm, the back of her neck,
and her knees.

It's true, she struggled at first, until after
the breaking. Then God was with her, and she
was with him.

What the Living Do

The Boy

My brother is walking down the sidewalk into the suburban summer night:
white T-shirt, blue jeans—to the field at the end of the street.

Hangers Hideout the boys called it, an undeveloped plot, a pit overgrown
with weeds, some old furniture thrown down there,

and some metal hangers clinking in the trees like wind chimes.
He's running away from home because our father wants to cut his hair.

And in two more days our father will convince me to go to him—you know
where he is—and talk to him: No reprisals. He promised.

A small parade of kids in feet pajamas will accompany me, their voices
like the first peepers in spring.   And my brother will walk ahead of us home,

and our father will shave his head bald, and my brother will not speak
to anyone the next month, not a word, not pass the milk, nothing.

What happened in our house taught my brothers how to leave, how to walk
down a sidewalk without looking back.

I was the girl. What happened taught me to follow him, whoever he was,
calling and calling his name.

Sixth Grade

The afternoon the neighborhood boys tied me and Mary Lou Maher
to Donny Ralph's father's garage doors, spread-eagled,
it was the summer they chased us almost every day.

Careening across the lawns they'd mowed for money,
on bikes they threw down, they'd catch us, lie on top of us,
then get up and walk away.

That afternoon Donny's mother wasn't home.
His nine sisters and brothers gone—even Gramps, who lived with them,
gone somewhere—the backyard empty, the big house quiet.

A gang of boys. They pulled the heavy garage doors down,
and tied us to them with clothesline,
and Donny got the deer's leg severed from the buck his dad had killed

the year before, dried up and still fur-covered, and sort of
poked it at us, dancing around the blacktop in his sneakers, laughing.
Then somebody took it from Donny and did it.

And then somebody else, and somebody after him.
Then Donny pulled up Mary Lou's dress and held it up,
and she began to cry, and I became a boy again, and shouted Stop,

and they wouldn't.
Then a girl-boy, calling out to Charlie, my best friend's brother,
who wouldn't look

Charlie! to my brother's friend who knew me
Stop them. And he wouldn't.
And then more softly, and looking directly at him, I said, Charlie.

And he said Stop. And they said What? And he said Stop it.
And they did, quickly untying the ropes, weirdly quiet,
Mary Lou still weeping. And Charlie? Already gone.

Buying the Baby

In those days you could buy a pagan baby for five dollars,
the whole class saved up. And when you bought it

you could name it Joseph, Mary, or Theresa, the class took a vote.
But on the day I brought in the five dollars

my grandmother had given me for my birthday something happened
—a fire drill? An assassination? And if it was announced

Marie Howe has, all by herself, bought a baby in India and gets to name it,
it was overshadowed and forgotten.

And if I tried to picture my baby, the CARE package
carried to her hut and placed before her, as her sisters and brothers watched,

that image dissolved into the long shining hall to the girls' lavatory.
Even in my own room, waiting for Roy Orbison to sing "Only the Lonely"

so I could sleep, I couldn't conjure that baby up.
The five dollars I gave her would never reach her. I knew that:

because I wanted my class to think me good for giving it.
Spiritual Pride the nuns called it, a Sin of Intention,

sister to the Sin of Omission, which was
the price for what you hadn't done but thought.

Sometimes I prayed so hard for God to materialize at the foot of my bed
it would start to happen;

then I'd beg it to stop, and it would.

Practicing

I want to write a love poem for the girls I kissed in seventh grade,
a song for what we did on the floor in the basement

of somebody's parents' house, a hymn for what we didn't say but thought:
That feels good or *I like that*, when we learned how to open each other's

mouths how to move our tongues to make somebody moan. We called it
practicing, and one was the boy, and we paired off—maybe six or eight girls,

and turned off the lights and kissed and kissed until we were stoned on kisses,
and lifted our nightgowns or let the straps drop, and, Now you be the boy:

concrete floor, sleeping bag, couch, playroom, game room, train room, laundry.
Linda's basement was like a boat with booths and portholes

instead of windows. Gloria's father had a bar downstairs with stools that
spun, plush carpeting. We kissed each other's throats.

We sucked each other's breasts, and we left marks, and never spoke of it
upstairs outdoors, in daylight, not once. We did it, and it was

practicing, and slept, sprawled so our legs still locked or crossed, a hand still
lost in someone's hair . . . and we grew up and hardly mentioned who

the first kiss really was—a girl like us, still sticky with moisturizer we'd
shared in the bathroom. I want to write a song

for that thick silence in the dark, and the first pure thrill of unreluctant
desire—just before we made ourselves stop.

The Attic

Praise to my older brother, the seventeen-year-old boy, who lived
in the attic with me an exiled prince grown hard in his confinement,

bitter, bent to his evening task building the imaginary building
on the drawing board they'd given him in school. His tools gleam

under the desk lamp. He is as hard as the pencil he holds,
drawing the line straight along the ruler.

Tower prince, young king, praise to the boy
who has willed his blood to cool and his heart to slow. He's building

a structure with so many doors it's finally quiet,
so that when our father climbs heavily up the attic stairs, he doesn't

at first hear him pass down the narrow hall. My brother is rebuilding
the foundation. He lifts the clear plastic of one page

to look more closely at the plumbing,
—he barely hears the springs of my bed when my father sits down—

he's imagining where the boiler might go, because
where it is now isn't working. Not until I've slammed the door behind

the man stumbling down the stairs again
does my brother look up from where he's working. I know it hurts him

to rise, to knock on my door and come in. And when he draws his skinny
arm around my shaking shoulders,

I don't know if he knows he's building a world where I can one day love a man—he sits there without saying anything.

Praise him.
I know he can hardly bear to touch me.

The Copper Beech

Immense, entirely itself,
it wore that yard like a dress,

with limbs low enough for me to enter it
and climb the crooked ladder to where

I could lean against the trunk and practice being alone.

One day, I heard the sound before I saw it, rain fell
darkening the sidewalk.

Sitting close to the center, not very high in the branches,
I heard it hitting the high leaves, and I was happy,

watching it happen without it happening to me.

The Game

And on certain nights,
maybe once or twice a year,
I'd carry the baby down
and all the kids would come
all nine of us together,
and we'd build a town in the basement

from boxes and blankets and overturned chairs.
And some lived under the pool table
or in the bathroom or the boiler room
or in the toy cupboard under the stairs,
and you could be a man or a woman
a husband or a wife or a child, and we bustled around
like a day in the village until

one of us turned off the lights, switch
by switch, and slowly it became night
and the people slept.

Our parents were upstairs with company or
not fighting, and one of us—it was usually
a boy—became the Town Crier,
and he walked around our little sleeping
population and tolled the hours with his voice,
and this was the game.

Nine o'clock and all is well, he'd say,
walking like a constable we must have seen
in a movie. And what we called an hour passed.

Ten o'clock and all is well.
And maybe somebody stirred in her sleep
or a grown up baby cried and was comforted . . .
Eleven o'clock and all is well.
Twelve o'clock. One o'clock. Two o'clock . . .

and it went on like that through the night we made up
until we could pretend it was morning.

The Girl

So close to the end of my childbearing life
without children

—if I could remember a day when I was utterly a girl
and not yet a woman—

but I don't think there was a day like that for me.

When I look at the girl I was, dripping in her bathing suit,
or riding her bike, pumping hard down the newly paved street,

she wears a furtive look—
and even if I could go back in time to her as me, the age I am now

she would never come into my arms
without believing that I wanted something.

The Dream

I had a dream in the day:
I laid my father's body down in a narrow boat

and sent him off along the riverbank with its cattails and grasses.
And the boat—it was made of bark and wood bent when it was wet—

took him to his burial finally.
But a day or two later I realized it was my self I wanted

to lay down, hands crossed, eyes closed . . .
Oh, the light coming up from down there,

the sweet smell of the water—and finally, the sense of being carried
by a current I could not name or change.

For Three Days

For three days now I've been trying to think of another word for gratitude
because my brother could have died and didn't,

because for a week we stood in the intensive care unit trying not to imagine
how it would be then, afterwards.

My youngest brother, Andy, said: This is so weird. I don't know if I'll be
talking with John today or buying a pair of pants for his funeral.

And I hated him for saying it because it was true and seemed to tilt it,
because I had been writing his elegy in my head during the seven-hour drive

and trying not to. Thinking meant not thinking. It meant imagining
my brother surrounded by light—like Schrödinger's Cat that would be dead

if you looked and might live if you didn't. And then it got better, and then
it got worse, and it's a story now: He came back.

And I did, by that time, imagine him dead. And I did begin to write the other
story: how the crowd in the stifling church snapped to a tearful attention,

how my brother lived again, for a few minutes, through me.
And although I know I couldn't help it, because fear has its own language

and its own story, because even grief provides a living remedy,
I can't help but think of that woman who said to him whom she considered

her savior: *If thou hadst been there my brother had not died*, how she might
have practiced her speech, and how she too might have stood trembling,

unable to meet the eyes of the dear familiar figure stumbling from the cave
when the compassionate fist of God opened

and crushed her with gratitude and shame.

Just Now

John opens his eyes when he hears the door click
open downstairs and Joe's steps walking up past the meowing cat,

and the second click of the upstairs door, and then he lifts
his face so that Joe can kiss him. Joe has brought armfuls

of broken magnolia branches in full blossom, and he putters
in the kitchen looking for a big jar to put them in and finds it.

And now they tower in the living room, white and sweet, where
John can see them if he leans out from his bed which

he can't do just now, and now Joe is cleaning, What a mess
you've left me, he says, and John is smiling, almost asleep again.

A Certain Light

He had taken the right pills the night before.
We had counted them out

from the egg carton where they were numbered so there'd be no mistake.
He had taken the morphine and the prednisone and the amitriptyline

and Florinef and Vancomycin and Halcion too quickly
and had thrown up in the bowl Joe had brought to the bed—a thin string

of blue spit—then waited a few minutes, to calm himself,
before he took them all again. And had slept through the night

and the morning and was still sleeping at noon—or not sleeping.
He was breathing maybe twice a minute, and we couldn't wake him,

we couldn't wake him until we shook him hard calling, John wake up now
John wake up—Who is the president?

And he couldn't answer.
His doctor told us we'd have to keep him up for hours.

He was all bones and skin, no tissue to absorb the medicine.
He couldn't walk unless two people held him.

And we made him talk about the movie: What was the best moment in
On the Waterfront? What was the music in Gone with the Wind?

And for seven hours he answered, if only to please us, mumbling
I like the morphine, sinking, rising, sleeping, rousing,

then only in pain again—but wakened.
So wakened that late that night in one of those still blue moments

that were a kind of paradise, he finally opened his eyes wide,
and the room filled with a certain light we thought we'd never see again.

Look at you two, he said. And we did.
And Joe said, Look at you.

And John said, How do I look?
And Joe said, Handsome.

How Some of It Happened

My brother was afraid, all his life, of going blind, so deeply
that he would turn the dinner knives away from, *looking at him,*

he said, as they lay on the kitchen table.
He would throw a sweatshirt over those knobs that lock the car door

from the inside, and once, he dismantled a chandelier in the middle
of the night when everyone was sleeping.

We found the pile of sharp and shining crystals in the upstairs hall.
So you understand, it was terrible

when they clamped his one eye open and put the needle in his cheek
and up and into his eye from underneath

and held it there for a full minute before they drew it slowly out
once a week for many weeks. He learned to *lean into it,*

to *settle down* he said, and still the eye went dead, ulcerated,
breaking up green in his head as the other eye, still blue

and wide open, looked and looked at the clock.

My brother promised me he wouldn't die after our father died.
He shook my hand on a train going home one Christmas and gave me

five years, as clearly as he promised he'd be home for breakfast when
I watched him walk into that New York City autumn night. *By nine, I promise,*

and he did come back. And five years later he gave me five years more.
So much for the brave pride of premonition,

the worry that won't let it happen.
You know, he said, I always knew I would die young.

And then I got sober, and I thought, OK, I'm not.
I'm going to see thirty and live to be an old man. And now

it turns out that I am going to die. Isn't that funny?

—One day it happens: what you have feared all your life,
the unendurably specific, the exact thing. No matter what you say or do.

This is what my brother said: Here, sit closer to the bed
so I can see you.

The Last Time

The last time we had dinner together in a restaurant
with white tablecloths, he leaned forward

and took my two hands in his and said,
I'm going to die soon. I want you to know that.

And I said, I think I do know.
And he said, What surprises me is that you don't.

And I said, I do. And he said, What?
And I said, Know that you're going to die.

And he said, No, I mean know that you are.

The Promise

In the dream I had when he came back not sick
but whole, and wearing his winter coat,

he looked at me as though he couldn't speak, as if
there were a law against it, a membrane he couldn't break.

His silence was what he could not
not do, like our breathing in this world, like our living,

as we do, in time.
And I told him: I'm reading all this Buddhist stuff,

and listen, we don't die when we die. Death is an event,
a threshold we pass through. We go on and on

and into light forever.
And he looked down, and then back up at me. It was the look we'd pass

across the table when Dad was drunk again and dangerous,
the level look that wants to tell you something,

in a crowded room, something important, and can't.

The Cold Outside

Soon I will die, he said—that was during the heat wave that summer:
the orange lilies bending toward the house beside the driveway,

the heater in his car broken on and blasting.
And the green shade flapped against the window screen,

as if what was out there inhaled and exhaled,
sliding away from the window, banging lightly against the sill,

sucked flat against the screen,
then peeling off and blowing out again.

Today the cold outside is bright and brittle,
heaps of hard snow between the sidewalk and the street,

and look, someone has shoveled a narrow path in front of the bakery,
so that, walking, a person has to step aside

and let another person through,
or pass through as the other person steps aside.

Soon I will die, he said, and then
what everyone has been afraid of for so long will have finally happened,

and then everyone can rest.

The Grave

That first summer I lay on the grass above it as if it were
a narrow bed, just my size,

lying on the ground above my brother's body like a log
floating on lake water above its own shadow.

* * *

During the first winter I drove there one afternoon
after Tom and Andy and Beth and Dor and Bahia had been there.

When I stepped out of the car their footprints marked the snowy lawn:
the men's big boots, the women's smaller ones,

and Bahia's little boot prints, as big as my hand, looping and falling down
into a snow angel next to his grave, then another messy angel on it,

and, a grave or two away, another one, and the little blotch where she got up
and brushed herself off. For some crazy reason I was wearing

high-heeled shoes in the snow, and, walking back to the car, they made
ovals and dots, fat exclamation marks,

walking inside the steps of my brothers and sisters.

* * *

One November, years later, I went there with Andy
who was, by then, as old as John was when he died,

as we lay on the frozen ground,
me, using my scarf as a pillow, on John's grave,

and Andy, on top of our father's grave, one grave away,
and we talked like that for a little while, companionably,

like an old couple talking in bed,
our eyes closed against the sunlight,

and when I cried, Andy didn't seem to wish me to stop, and that
was a kind of happiness,

lying there with my living brother, talking about our family.
The ground was cold.

Eventually the chill crept through our coats and jeans and
we scuffled up—Andy reached down

to give me his hand—and then it was over.
We walked together back to the car and away from them.

The Gate

I had no idea that the gate I would step through
to finally enter this world

would be the space my brother's body made. He was
a little taller than me: a young man

but grown, himself by then,
done at twenty-eight, having folded every sheet,

rinsed every glass he would ever rinse under the cold
and running water.

This is what you have been waiting for, he used to say to me.
And I'd say, What?

And he'd say, This—holding up my cheese and mustard sandwich.
And I'd say, What?

And he'd say, This, sort of looking around.

One of the Last Days

As through a door in the air that I stepped through sideways
before reaching for a plate high in the cupboard

I find myself in the middle of my life: May night, raining,
Michael just gone to Provincetown, James making music next door,

lilacs in full bloom, sweet in the dark rain of Cambridge.

On one of the last days I told him, You know how much you love Joe?
That's how much I love you. And he said, No. And I said, Yes.

And he said, No. And I said, You know it's true.
And he closed his eyes for a minute.

When he opened them he said, Maybe you better start looking
for somebody else.

Late Morning

I was still in my white nightgown and James had drawn me down
to sit on his lap, and I was looking over his shoulder through the hall

into the living room, and he was looking over my shoulder, into the trees
through the open window I imagine,

and we sat like that for a few minutes, without saying much of anything,
my cheek pressed lightly

against his cheek, and my brother John was dead.
Suddenly close and distinct, it seemed finished, as if time were a room

I could gaze clear across—four years since I'd lifted his hand from
the sheets on his bed and cooled it in my hand.

A light breeze through the open window, James's warm cheek,
a brightness in the windy trees as I remember, crumbs and dishes still

on the table, and a small glass bottle of milk and an open jar of
raspberry jam.

Watching Television

I didn't want to look at the huge white egg the mother spider dragged
along behind her, attached to her abdomen, held off the ground,

bigger than her own head—
and inside it: hundreds of baby spiders feeding off the nest,

and, in what seemed like the next minute,
spinning their own webs quickly and crazily,

bumping into each other's and breaking them, then mending
and moving over, and soon they got it right:

each in his or her own circle and running around it.
And then they slept,

each in the center of a glistening thing: a red dot in ether.

Last night the moon was as big as a house at the end of the street,
a white frame house, and rising,

and I thought of a room it was shining in, right then,
a room I might live in and can't imagine yet.

And this morning, I thought of a place on the ocean where no one is,
no boat, no fish jumping,

just sunlight gleaming on the water, humps of water that hardly break.

I have argued bitterly with the man I love, and for two days
we haven't spoken.

We argued about one thing, but really it was another.
I keep finding myself by the front windows looking out at the street

and the walk that leads to the front door of this building,
white, unbroken by footprints.

Anything I've ever tried to keep by force I've lost.

Separation

Driving out of town, I see him crossing
the Brooks Pharmacy parking lot, and remember

how he would drop to his knees in the kitchen
and press his face to my dress, his cheek flat against

my belly as if he were listening for something.
Somebody might be waiting for coffee in the living room,

someone might be setting the dining room table, he'd
place his face under my dress and press his cheek

against my belly and kneel there, without saying anything.
How is it possible that I am allowed to see him

like this—walking quickly by the glass windows?

—what he wears in the world without me,
his hands swinging by his side, his cock quiet

in his jeans, his shirt covering
his shoulders, his own tongue in his mouth.

Prayer

Someone or something is leaning close to me now
trying to tell me the one true story of my life:

one note,
low as a bass drum, beaten over and over:

It's beginning summer,
and the man I love has forgotten my smell

the cries I made when he touched me, and my laughter
when he picked me up

and carried me, still laughing, and laid me down,
among the scattered daffodils on the dining room table.

And Jane is dead,
                            and I want to go where she went,
where my brother went,

and whoever it is that whispered to me

when I was a child in my father's bed is come back now:
and I can't stop hearing:
                            This is the way it is,
the way it always was and will be—

beaten over and over—panicking on street corners,
or crouched in the back of taxicabs,

afraid I'll cry out in jammed traffic, and no one will know me or
know where to bring me.

There is, I almost remember,
another story:

It runs alongside this one like a brook beside a train.
The sparrows know it; the grass rises with it.

The wind moves through the highest tree branches without
seeming to hurt them.

Tell me.
Who was I when I used to call your name?

Reunion

The very best part was rowing out onto the small lake in a little boat:

James and I taking turns fishing, one fishing as the other rowed slowly—
the long sigh of the line through the air,

and the far plunk of the hook and the sinker—
lily pads, yellow flowers

the dripping of the oars
and the knock and creak of them moving in the rusty locks.

The Kiss

When he finally put
his mouth on me—on

my shoulder the world
shifted a little on the tilted

axis of itself. The minutes
since my brother died

stopped marching ahead like
dumb soldiers and

the stars rested.
His mouth on my shoulder and

then on my throat
and the world started up again

for me,
some machine deep inside it

recalibrating,
all the little wheels

slowly reeling then speeding up,
the massive dawn lifting on the other

side of the turning world.
And when his mouth

pressed against my
mouth, I

opened my mouth
and the world's chord

played at once:
a large, ordinary music rising

from a hand neither one of us could see.

My Dead Friends

I have begun,
when I'm weary and can't decide an answer to a bewildering question

to ask my dead friends for their opinion
and the answer is often immediate and clear.

Should I take the job? Move to the city? Should I try to conceive a child
in my middle age?

They stand in unison shaking their heads and smiling—whatever leads
to joy, they always answer,

to more life and less worry. I look into the vase where Billy's ashes were—
it's green in there, a green vase,

and I ask Billy if I should return the difficult phone call, and he says, yes.
Billy's already gone through the frightening door,

whatever he says I'll do.

What the Living Do

Johnny, the kitchen sink has been clogged for days, some utensil probably
   fell down there.
And the Drano won't work but smells dangerous, and the crusty dishes have
   piled up

waiting for the plumber I still haven't called. This is the everyday we spoke
   of.
It's winter again: the sky's a deep headstrong blue, and the sunlight pours
   through

the open living room windows because the heat's on too high in here, and I
   can't turn it off.
For weeks now, driving, or dropping a bag of groceries in the street, the bag
   breaking,

I've been thinking: This is what the living do. And yesterday, hurrying along
   those
wobbly bricks in the Cambridge sidewalk, spilling my coffee down my wrist
   and sleeve,

I thought it again, and again later, when buying a hairbrush: This is it.
   Parking.
Slamming the car door shut in the cold. What you called *that yearning.*

What you finally gave up. We want the spring to come and the winter to
   pass. We want
whoever to call or not call, a letter, a kiss—we want more and more and
   then more of it.

But there are moments, walking, when I catch a glimpse of myself in the
   window glass,

say, the window of the corner video store, and I'm gripped by a cherishing
   so deep

for my own blowing hair, chapped face, and unbuttoned coat that I'm
   speechless:
I am living, I remember you.

Buddy

Andy sees us to the door, and Buddy is suddenly all over him, leaping
and barking because Andy said walk. Are you going to walk home? He said.

To me. And Buddy thinks him and now, and he's wrong. He doesn't
understand the difference between sign and symbol like we do—the thing

and the word for the thing. How we can talk about something when it's not
even there, without it actually happening—the way I talk about John.

Andy meant: soon. He meant me. As for Buddy, Andy meant: later. When he
was good and ready, he said. Buddy doesn't understand. He's in a state

of agitation and grief, scratching at the door. If one of us said, Andy,
when Andy wasn't there, that silly Buddy would probably jump up barking

and begin looking for him.

The Kingdom of
Ordinary Time

■

The Star Market

The people Jesus loved were shopping at The Star Market yesterday.
An old lead-colored man standing next to me at the checkout
breathed so heavily I had to step back a few steps.

Even after his bags were packed he stood still, breathing hard and
hawking into his hand. The feeble, the lame, I could hardly look at them:
shuffling through the aisles, they smelled of decay, as if The Star Market

had declared a day off for the able-bodied, and I had wandered in
with the rest of them: sour milk, bad meat:
looking for cereal and spring water.

Jesus must have been a saint, I said to myself, looking for my lost car
in the parking lot later, stumbling among the people who would have
been lowered into rooms by ropes, who would have crept

out of caves or crawled from the corners of public baths on their hands
and knees begging for mercy.

If I touch only the hem of his garment, one woman thought,
Could I bear the look on his face when he wheels around?

Reading Ovid

The thing about those Greeks and Romans is that
    at least mythologically,

they could get mad. If the man broke your heart, if he
    raped your sister speechless

then real true hell broke loose:
    "You know that stew you just ate for dinner, honey?—

It was your son."
    That's Ovid for you.

A guy who knows how to tell a story about people who
    really don't believe in the Golden Rule.

Sometimes, I fantasize about saying to the man I married, "You know
    that hamburger you just

gobbled down with relish and mustard? It was
    your truck."

If only to watch understanding take his face
    like the swan-god took the girl.

But rage makes for more rage—nothing to do then but run.
    And because rage is a story that has

no ending, we'd both have to transform into birds or fish:
    constellations forever fixed

in the starry heavens, forever separated,
    forever attached.

Remember the story of Athens and Sparta?
       That boy held the fox under his cloak

and didn't flinch. A cab driver told me the part
       I couldn't remember this morning—

in Sparta, he said, it was permissible to steal
       but not get caught.

The fox bit and scratched; the kid didn't talk,
       and he was a hero.

Do unto others as you would have them do unto you,
       Jesus said. He said, The kingdom of heaven

is within you.
       And the spiked wheel ploughed through the living centuries

minute by minute, soul by soul. Ploughs still. That's the good news
       and the bad news, isn't it?

After the Movie

My friend Michael and I are walking home arguing about the movie. He says
that he believes a person can love someone and still be able to murder that person.

I say, No, that's not love. That's attachment.
Michael says, No, that's love. You can love someone, then come to a day

when you're forced to think "it's him or me"
think "me" and kill him.

I say, Then it's not love anymore.
Michael says, It was love up to then though.

I say, Maybe we mean different things by the same word.
Michael says, Humans are complicated.
                        Love can exist even in the murderous heart.

I say that what he might mean by love is desire.
Love is not a feeling, I say. And Michael says, Then what is it?

We're walking along West 16th Street—a clear unclouded night—and I hear
my voice repeating what I used to say to my husband:
                        Love is action, I used to say to him.

Simone Weil says that when you really love you are able to look at
someone you want to eat and not eat them.

Janis Joplin says, take another little piece of my heart now baby.

Meister Eckhardt says that as long as we love any image
                        we are doomed to live in purgatory.

Michael and I stand on the corner of 6th Avenue saying goodnight.
I can't drink enough of the tangerine spritzer I've just bought—

again and again I bring the cold can to my mouth and suck the stuff from
the hole the flip top made.

What are you doing tomorrow? Michael says.
But what I think he's saying is "You are too strict. You are a nun."

Then I think, Do I love Michael enough to allow him to think these things
of me even if he's not thinking them?

Above Manhattan, the moon wanes, and the sky turns clearer and colder.
Although the days, after the solstice, have started to lengthen,

we both know the winter has only begun.

Limbo

Each of them can't decide if there is a God
or if there is a self.

Do I have an I? one says
to another who seems distracted,
        looking out what might have been a window.

What is the difference between a self and a soul?
Is it true that one god is in a relationship to each of us?
Or is the each of us an illusion, and we are the god we are looking for?
        That's what the distracted one is thinking and what
she wants to know,

and she wishes that other person would stop bothering her,
and she wishes she had more time to think about these things,
although she has all the time in the world.

Easter

Two of the fingers on his right hand
had been broken

so when he poured back into that hand it surprised
him—it hurt him at first.

And the whole body was too small. Imagine
the sky trying to fit into a tunnel carved into a hill.

He came into it two ways:
From the outside, as we step into a pair of pants.

And from the center—suddenly all at once.
Then he felt himself awake in the dark alone.

Marriage

My husband likes to watch the cooking shows, the building shows,
the Discovery Channel, and the surgery channel.
Last night he told us about a man who came into the emergency room

with a bayonet stuck entirely through his skull and brain.
Did they get it out? We all asked.
They did. And the man was ok because the blade went exactly between

the two halves without severing them.
And who had shoved this bayonet into the man's head? His wife.
A strong woman, someone said. And everyone else agreed.

Prayer

Every day I want to speak with you.
And every day something more important calls for my attention

—the drugstore, the beauty products, the luggage
I need to buy for the trip.

Even now I can hardly sit here
among the falling piles of paper and clothing,
the garbage trucks outside already screeching and banging.

The mystics say you are as close as my own breath.
Why do I flee from you?

My days and nights pour through me like complaints
and become a story I forgot to tell.

Help me. Even as I write these words I am planning
to rise from the chair as soon as I finish this sentence.

Courage

I'm helping my little girl slide down the pole
next to the slide-and-bridge construction when a little boy walks up and says,

Why are you helping that young person do something that's too dangerous for her?

Why do you say it's too dangerous? I say
And he says, She's too young.
And I say, How old are you? And he says, four and a half.
And I say, Well, she's three and a half

When he comes back a little later he says, I'll show you how it's done, and
climbs up the ladder and slides down the pole.

Then he says, She's too young.
What happens is that when you get older you get braver.

Then he pauses and looks at me, Are you brave?
Brave? I say, looking at him.

Are you afraid of Parasite 2? he says.
And I say, What's Parasite 2?
And he walks away slowly, shaking his head.

Why the Novel Is Necessary but Sometimes Hard to Read

It happens in time. *Years passed until the old woman,*
one snowy morning, realized she has never loved her daughter . . .

Or, *Five years later she answered the door, and her suitor had returned*
almost unrecognizable from his journeys . . .

But before you get to that part you have to learn the names
you have to suffer not knowing anything about anyone

and slowly come to understand who each of them is, or who each of them
imagines him or her self to be—

and then, because you are the reader, you must try to understand who
you think each of them is because of who you believe yourself to be

in relation to their situation
or your memory of one very much like it.

Oh it happens in time and time is hard to live through.
I can't read anything anymore, my dying brother said one afternoon,
not even letters. Come on, Come on, he said, waving his hand in the air,
What am I interested in—plot?

You come upon the person the author put there
as if you'd been pushed into a room and told to watch the dancing—

pushed into pantries, into basements, across moors, into
the great drawing rooms of great cities, into the small cold cabin, or

to here, beside the small running river where a boy is weeping,
and no one comes,

and you have to watch without saying anything he can hear.

One by one the readers come and watch him weeping by the running river, and he never knows,

unless he too has read the story where a boy feels himself all alone.

This is the life you have written, the novel tells us. *What happens next?*

Government

Standing next to my old friend I sense that his soldiers have retreated.
And mine? They're resting their guns on their shoulders
talking quietly.   I'm hungry, one says.
Cheeseburger, says another,
and they all decide to go and find some dinner.

But the next day, negotiating the too narrow aisles of
The Health and Harmony Food Store—when I say, Excuse me,
to the woman with her cart of organic chicken and green grapes
she pulls the cart not quite far back enough for me to pass,
and a small mob in me begins picking up the fruit to throw.

So many kingdoms,
and in each kingdom, so many people; the disinherited son,
the corrupt counselor, the courtesan, the fool.

And so many gods—arguing among themselves,
over toast, through the lunch salad
and on into the long hours of the mild spring afternoon—I'm the god.
No, I'm the god. No, I'm the god.

I can hardly hear myself talking over their muttering.
How can I discipline my army? They're exhausted and want more money.
How can I disarm when my enemy seems so intent?

Poems from the Life of Mary

Sometimes the moon sat in the well at night.
And when I stirred it with a stick it broke.
If I kept stirring it swirled like white
water, as if water were light, and the stick
a wand that made the light follow, then slow
into water again, un-wobbling, until
the wind moved it.
                        And I thought of all the moons
floating over the wells and rivers, spilling
over rocks where the water broke: moons
in the sheep water, the chicken water,
Or here or there an oar bent it, or a woman
spread out her skirt and let it pool there—
the light I mean, not the moon in a circle, not
the moon itself, but the light that fell from it.

Once or twice or three times, I saw something
rise from the dust in the yard, like the soul
of the dust, or from the field, the soul-body
of the field—rise and hover like a veil in the sun
billowing—as if I could see the wind itself.
I thought I did it—squinting—but I didn't.
As if the edges of things blurred—so what was in
bled out, breathed up and mingled: bush and cow
and dust and well: breathed a field I walked through
waist high, as through high grass or water, my fingers
swirling through it—or it through me. I saw it.
It was thing and spirit both: the real
world: evident, invisible.

How you can't move moonlight—you have to go
there and stand in it. How you can't coax it
from your bed to come and shine there. You can't
carry it in a bucket or cup it in
your hands to drink it. Wind won't

blow it. A bird flying through it won't
tear it. How you can't sell it or buy it
or save it or earn it or own it, erase
it or block it from shining on the mule's
bristly back, dog's snout, duck bill, cricket, toad.
Shallow underwater stones gleam underwater.

And the man who's just broken the neck
of his child? He's standing by the window
moonlight shining on his face and throat.

You think this happened only once and long ago?
Think of a summer night and someone
talking across the water,
                                    maybe someone
you loved in a boat, rowing. And you could
hear the oars dripping in the water, from
half a lake away, and they were far and
close at once. You didn't need to touch them
or call to them or talk about it later.
—the sky? It was what you breathed. The lake?
sky that fell as rain. I have been like you
filled with worry, worry—then relief.
You know the wind is sky moving. It happens all the time.

Annunciation

Even if I don't see it again—nor ever feel it
I know it is—and that if it once hailed me
it ever does—

And so it is myself I want to turn in that direction
not as towards a place, but it was a tilting
within myself,

as one turns a mirror to flash the light to where
it isn't—I was blinded like that—and swam
in what shone at me

only able to endure it by being no one and so
specifically myself I thought I'd die
from being loved like that.

My Mother's Body

Bless my mother's body, the first song of her beating
heart and her breathing, her voice, which I could dimly hear,

grew louder. From inside her body I heard almost every word she said.
Within that girl I drove to the store and back, her feet pressing

the pedals of the blue car, her voice, first gate to the cold sunny mornings,
rain, moonlight, snow fall, dogs . . .

Her kidneys failed, the womb where I once lived is gone.
Her young, astonished body pushed me down that long corridor,

and my body hurt her, I know that—she was 24 years old. I'm old enough
to be that girl's mother, to smooth her hair, to look

into her exultant frightened eyes, her bedsheets stained with chocolate,
her heart in constant failure. It's a girl, someone must have said.

She must have kissed me with her mouth, first grief, first air,
and soon I was drinking her, first food, I was eating my mother,

slumped in her wheelchair, one of my brothers pushing it,
across the snowy lawn, her eyes fixed, her face averted.

Bless this body she made, my long legs, her long arms and fingers,
our voice in my throat speaking to you now.

Before the Fire

Last night I lay on the floor of my friend's living room
and watched the burning cinders sift from the grate to the fireplace floor.

How good it was to look into the indifferent element.
What is fire, my friend said. Is it the log? Something different from the log?

is it the log consuming itself? We lay there, adding one log after another
until the fire was ash.

My soul drank enough to know how thirsty it was.
This morning, the sunlight falling to the far corner of the bed, I remember

the dream of the forked stick—the divining stick that can find water. . . .
Susan, my old friend, put it into my hands, and I started across the yard

thinking to pretend to find what she wanted. But at a certain point
It pulled so hard I had to hold on, it pulled so hard towards the ground.

Fifty

The soul has a story that has a shape that almost no one
sees. No, no one ever does. All those kisses,

The bedroom chair that rocked with me in it, his body
his body and his and his and his.
                                        More, I said, more
and more and more. . . . What has it come to?
Like dresses I tried on and dropped to the floor. . . .

Hurry

We stop at the dry cleaners and the grocery store
and the gas station and the green market and
Hurry up honey, I say, hurry,
as she runs along two or three steps behind me
her blue jacket unzipped and her socks rolled down.

Where do I want her to hurry to? To her grave?
To mine? Where one day she might stand all grown?
Today, when all the errands are finally done, I say to her,
Honey I'm sorry I keep saying Hurry—
you walk ahead of me. You be the mother.

And, Hurry up, she says, over her shoulder, looking
back at me, laughing. Hurry up now darling, she says,
hurry, hurry, taking the house keys from my hands.

The Spell

(In Memory of Elise Asher)

Our four-year-old neighbor Pablo has lost his wand
and so he tries to cast spells with his finger
which doesn't seem to work as well.

Then he brings handfuls of dimes and nickels to the couch
where I'm sitting, and when I say, Give me some money,
he says, No, laughing.

Give me some money, I say,
and he says, No.

Then he draws, on a piece of paper, a circle with a 10 inside
the word No, an unhappy mouth and eyes,
and gives that to me.

Why not ask the wand to find itself?
No, he says, shaking his head slowly.
Why not make a spell that will find it?
No, he says, that won't work.
What about this stick? His mother says, holding up a chopstick.
No, says Pablo, who knows the difference between what is secular and
what is sacred.

Every day when I pick up my four-year-old daughter from preschool
she climbs into her back booster seat and says, Mom—tell me your story.
And almost every day I tell her: I dropped you off, I taught my class
I ate a tuna fish sandwich, wrote e-mails, returned phone calls, talked
with students, and then I came to pick you up.

And almost every day I think, My God, is that what I did?

Yesterday, she climbed into the backseat and said, Mom
tell me your story, and I did what I always did:
        I said I dropped you off
taught my class, had lunch, returned e-mails, talked with students. . . .
        And she said, No Mom, tell me the whole thing.

And I said, ok. I feel a little sad.
And she said, Tell me the whole thing Mom.
And I said, ok Elise died.

Elise is dead and the world feels weary and brokenhearted.
And she said, Tell me the whole thing Mom.
And I said, in my dream last night I felt my life building up around me and
        when I stepped forward and away from it and turned around I saw
        a high and frozen crested wave.

        And she said, the whole thing Mom.
Then I thought of the other dream, I said, when a goose landed on my head—
But when I'd untangled it from my hair I saw it wasn't a goose
but a winged serpent writhing up into the sky like a disappearing bee.

And she said, Tell me the whole story.
And I said, Elise is dead, and all the frozen tears are mine, of course
and if that wave broke it might wash my life clear,
                and I might begin again from now and from here.

And I looked into the rearview mirror—
She was looking sideways, out the window, to the right
                                —where they say the unlived life is.
Ok? I said.
And she said, Ok, still looking in that direction.

The Snow Storm

I walked down towards the river, and the deer had left tracks
deep as half my arm, that ended in a perfect hoof
and the shump shump sound my boots made walking made the silence loud.

And when I turned back towards the great house
I walked beside the deer tracks again.
And when I came near the feeder: little tracks of the birds on the surface
        of the snow I'd broken through.

Put your finger here, and see my hands,
                        then bring your hand and put it in my side.

I put my hand down into the deer track
                        and touched the bottom of an invisible hoof,

then my finger in the little mark of the jay.

Mary (Reprise)

What is that book we always see—in the painting—in her lap?
Her finger keeping the place of who she was when she looked up?

When I look up: my mother is dead, and my own daughter is calling
from the bathtub, Mom come in and watch me—come in here right now!

No Going Back might be the name of that angel—no more reverie.
Let it be done to me, Mary finally said, and that

was the last time, for a long time, that she spoke about the past.

Magdalene

His disciples said, When will you be visible to us?
and when will we see you?
He said, When you undress and are not ashamed.

—T h e G o s p e l A c c o r d i n g t o T h o m a s

Before the Beginning

Was I ever virgin?

Did someone touch me before I could speak?

Who had me before I knew I was an I?

So that I wanted that touch again and again

without knowing who or why or from whence it came?

Magdalene—The Seven Devils

"Mary, called Magdalene, from whom seven devils had been cast out" (*Luke* 8:2)

The first was that I was very busy.

The second—I was different from you: whatever happened to you could

not happen to me, not like that.

The third—I worried.

The fourth—envy, disguised as compassion.

The fifth was that I refused to consider the quality of life of the aphid,

The aphid disgusted me. But I couldn't stop thinking about it.

The mosquito too—its face.   And the ant—its trifurcated body.

Ok   the first was that I was so busy.

The second that I might make the wrong choice,

because I had decided to take that plane that day,

that flight, before noon, so as to arrive early

and, I shouldn't have wanted that.

The third was that if I walked past the certain place on the street

the house would blow up.

The fourth was that I was made of guts and blood with a thin layer

of skin lightly thrown over the whole thing.

The fifth was that the dead seemed more alive to me than the living.

The sixth—if I touched my right arm I had to touch my left arm, and if I

touched the left arm a little harder than I'd first touched the right then I had

to retouch the left and then touch the right again so it would be even.

The seventh—I knew I was breathing the expelled breath of everything that

was alive, and I couldn't stand it.

I wanted a sieve, a mask, a, I hate this word—cheesecloth—

to breath through that would trap it—whatever was inside everyone else that

entered me when I breathed in.

No. That was the first one.

The second was that I was so busy. I had no time. How had this happened?

How had our lives gotten like this?

The third was that I couldn't eat food if I really saw it—distinct, separate

from me in a bowl or on a plate.

Ok. The first was that. I could never get to the end of the list.

The second was that the laundry was never finally done.

The third was that no one knew me, although they thought they did.

And that if people thought of me as little as I thought of them then

what was love?

The fourth was I didn't belong to anyone. I wouldn't allow myself

to belong to anyone.

The fifth was that I knew none of us could ever know what we didn't know.

The sixth was that I projected onto others what I myself was feeling.

The seventh was the way my mother looked when she was dying,

the sound she made—her mouth wrenched to the right and cupped open

so as to take in as much air . . . the gurgling sound, so loud

we had to speak louder to hear each other over it.

And that I couldn't stop hearing it—

years later—grocery shopping, crossing the street—

No, not the sound—it was her body's hunger

finally evident—what our mother had hidden all her life.

For months I dreamt of knucklebones and roots,

the slabs of sidewalk pushed up like crooked teeth

by what grew underneath.

The underneath. That was the first devil. It was always with me.

And that I didn't think you—if I told you—would understand any of this—

On Men, Their Bodies

One penis was very large and thick so when he put it inside me I really did

say, Wow. One penis was uncircumcised, and I loved to grip the shaft and

pull down so the head popped out like a little man. One penis was curved so

I had to move in a different way. One penis was so friendly I was never

afraid of it. One penis was so slender I was startled. One penis was blunt

and short. One penis couldn't harden until he stuffed it soft inside me. One

penis came as soon as I started to move. I'm so sorry, he said, I have a

problem, but I didn't care. I loved that boy. One penis pressed against me

hard almost every morning, but I got out of bed as if I hadn't heard a word it

said. One penis was so dear to me I kissed it and kissed it even after I knew

it had been with someone else. One penis I never saw, but my hand came to

know it from the outside of his jeans. One penis loved the inside of my mouth

so much it sang, it sputtered. One had a name. One was a mouse. One, he

explained to me, had very tiny crabs, so we couldn't have sex for a while.

One was Orthodox and wouldn't touch blood. One had a mole, a hard little

dot just under the rim. One penis was extremely patient without making a big deal about it. One penis had a great sense of humor. One penis had herpes

but I didn't know that word yet. One was a battering ram. One was a drunk

staggering, a lout, a bully. One slept inside me, comfortably at home.

How the Story Started

I was driven toward desire by desire

believing that fulfillment of that desire was an end.

There was no end.

Others might have looked into the future and seen

a shape inside the coming years—

a house, a child, a man who might be a help.

I saw his back bent over what he was working on,

the back of his neck, how he stood in his sneakers,

and wanted to eat him.

How could I see another person, I mean who *he* was—apart from me—

apart from that?

Thorns

I pressed them through my hair into my head

pressed them into my waistband and

later into my palms,

a secret intimacy among those thorns and me

a love

(from whom or to whom it mattered less than

that it was) and that

it was

was the evidence of love:

and so a comfort in the small

pain they brought.

The Affliction

When I walked across a room, I saw myself walking

as if I were someone else,

when I picked up a fork, pulled off a dress,

as if I were in a movie.

It's what I thought you saw when you looked at me.

So when I looked at you, I didn't see you

I saw the me I thought you saw, as if I were someone else.

I called that *outside*—watching. Well I didn't call it anything

when it happened all the time.

But one morning after I stopped the pills—standing in the kitchen

for one second I was *inside* looking out.

Then I popped back outside. And saw myself looking.

Would it happen again? It did—a few days later.

My friend Wendy was pulling on her coat, standing by the kitchen door

and suddenly I was *inside* and I saw her.

I looked out from my own eyes

and I saw her eyes: blue gray   transparent

and inside them: Wendy herself!

Then I was outside again.

and Wendy was saying, Bye-bye, see you soon,

as if Nothing Had Happened.

She hadn't noticed. She hadn't known that I'd Been There

for Maybe 40 Seconds,

and that I was Gone.

She hadn't noticed that I Hadn't Been There for Months

years, the entire time she'd known me.

I needn't have been embarrassed to have been there for those seconds;

she had not Noticed The Difference.

This happened on and off for weeks,

and then I was looking at my old friend John:

: suddenly I was in: and I saw him,

and he: (and this was almost unbearable)

he saw me see him,

and I saw him see me.

He said something like, You're going to be ok now,

or, It's been difficult hasn't it,

but what he said mattered only a little.

We met—in our mutual gaze—in between:

a third place I'd not yet been.

Magdalene: The Addict

I liked Hell,

I liked to go there alone

relieved to lie in the wreckage, ruined, physically undone.

The worst had happened. What else could hurt me then?

I thought it was the worst, thought nothing worse could come.

Then nothing did, and no one.

The Landing

I stood beside the high cupboard that covered

the radiator in the hall (inside the drawers: the odd pencils and pins

we couldn't find when we needed them)

near the front stairs that rose up and turned by the high windows.

What did we call that space? The landing.

All the pills had brought me to that place

And I understood that if I kept it all up . . .

no one would know me.

A dim light far in the distance? No.

To love—I had to be there.

I had to be there to be loved.

The Teacher

When Moses pleaded, and Yaweh agreed at last to let the people

hear His voice,

it's said that he allowed each person to hear what each could bear

to the very brim of that and no more.

Afterwards the people said, Please Moses, from now on you listen.

We don't want to hear it. You do the talking and listening now.

Being with the teacher was a little like that

as though he were a book too difficult to read.

So, I thought I had to become more than I was, more than I'd been.

but that wasn't it. It seemed rather that

something had to go. Something had to be let go of.

It wasn't that I saw something new—or saw suddenly into him,

not that, not ever

but the room itself, whatever room we might be standing in,

assumed an astonishing clarity:

and the things in the room: a table, a cup, a meowing cat.

The Disciples

I suppose it's always like that with a teacher.

Everyone wanted his gaze as if it were water at noon.

But it was women who made the food,

women who opened their homes to us,

their quiet daughters standing in the doorway,

the little ones being told to let him rest, let him eat,

and they hadn't cooked a dish.

It was still the old way

although they all talked about the new way, the new way.

For me it was different.

I knew that even when he seemed not to be looking at me, he was.

But of course I was wrong about that too.

Magdalene on Gethsemane

When he went to the garden the night before

And fell with his face to the ground

what he imagined was not his torture, not his own death

       That's what the story says, but that's not what he told me.

He said he saw the others *the countless* in his name

raped, burned, lynched, stoned, bombed, beheaded, shot, gassed,

gutted and raped again.

Calvary

Someone hanging clothes on a line between buildings,

someone shaking out a rug from an open window

might have heard hammering, one or two blocks away

and thought little or nothing of it.

Low Tide, Late August

That last summer when everything was almost always terrible

we waded into the bay one late afternoon as the tide had almost finished

pulling all the way out

and sat down in the waist-deep water

I, on his lap, facing him, my legs floating around him,

and we quietly coupled,

and stayed loosely joined like that, not moving,

but being moved by the softly sucking and lapping water,

as the pulling out reached its limit,
                    and the tide began to flow slowly back again.

Some children ran after each other, squealing in the shallows,
                              near but not too near.

I rested my chin on his shoulder looking toward the shore,

as he must have been looking over my shoulder,

to where the water deepened

and the small boats tugged on their anchors.

The Adoption: When the Girl Arrived

She took me from the place in the center where it was quiet,

where time falls as sunlight through a gauze curtain

and the animal in me slept and dreamed and stirred

(—a sleeping animal, running)

She pulled me from desire for a shoulder or a back

                                        a body pressed to my body

She pulled me from prayer and desire

                            from even the memory

the smell and sound of him moaning against me

the dark warm cave of want filled and filled and filled—stuffed

overstuffed.   That stopped.

Conversation: Dualism

Is that bad? the girl says, when someone tells a story, or when we see

an accident on the road, or lately when almost anything happens.

Well, I say, not good, nor bad.

But is it bad? she says again, sensing my small

hesitation. Well,

not good, I say

—and that seals it.

The News

The girls in their booster seats behind me are playing mermaids.

Hey mother mermaid! they call out—

I'm listening to the car radio: the senator breaking down on the senate floor,

speaking against his party's nomination to the United Nations,

and I say Yes my mermaids, what is it? as the senator says,

My colleagues tell me, Don't worry,

        but I think of my children, and my grandchildren

(And here he actually begins sobbing)

        We're dead! The girls shout from the back

You're what? I say, Dead! They call out laughing. Be sad.

Boo hoo, I say, They're dead, I'm sad (still listening to the senator)

and then a sighing sort of singing comes from the back seat,

Wooooooooooo, we're spirits, the girls sing

—high and sweet as the lost song of a lost race—

and then—Now we're back!   Laughing, and dying

and coming back maybe half a dozen more times

before I pull into their preschool driveway and stop.

This chamber, the senator says, is ominously quiet.

Then one of the girls says, Now let's just one of us be dead.

And the other says, Ok.

And first girl says, Who? And the other says, You.

and the rest is history.

Walking Home

Everything dies, I said. How had that started?

A tree? The winter? Not me, she said.

And I said, Oh yeah? And she said, I'm reincarnating.

Ha, she said, See you in a few thousand years!

Why years, I wondered, why not minutes? Days?

She found that so funny—Ha Ha—doubled over—

Years, she said, confidently.

I think you and I have known each other a few lifetimes, I said.

She said, I have never before been a soul on this earth.

(It was cold. We were hungry.) Next time, you be the mother, I said.

No way, Jose, she said, as we turned the last windy corner.

The Map

The failure of love might account for most of the suffering in the world.

The girl was going over her global studies homework in the air

where she drew the map with her finger

              touching the Gobi Desert,

the Plateau of Tiber in front of her,

and looking through her transparent map backwards

I did suddenly see,

how her left is my right, and for a moment I understood.

Waiting at the River

Sometimes, I'm tired of being a mother, weary of holding her in my mind, her words brighter than mine, the light's movement on the rock. Look, I say, Listen, to what my daughter said. (Tired of being) Reasonable and calm, answering to Mom, and how sweet (the sound) my name in her mouth, her mouth on my name, her mouth is not my mouth, her mind (not my). Her body has too many bites on it (too many) scratched. I'm the post she touches and leaves, and (before she) leaves (I'm) the base she runs to, and pushes off from: transparent home, ignored, rebuilt, undone, restored (all) without her knowing, waiting to catch the shine off her hair as she rounds the (watery) bend in the river, stepping among the stones. I stand up (waving), stretch and stand up, to show her where I am.

Christmas Eve

When I brought the girl to bed

    earlier in the evening when the guests were still there

I'd noticed that the little manger we'd set up on the side table was empty—

    green light from the small bulb shining into empty space.

Later when I went to check on her, I saw she'd built a labyrinth of blocks,

    a very high tower in the center of the labyrinth

and on the top of this tower—an angel on its back,

    and at the foot of the tower—the clay baby Jesus and a lamb.

Where was Mary and Joseph?

Here, she pointed out from her bed—wandering through the seemingly

    endless corridors of the labyrinth—looking for their lost child.

Two Animals

This morning walking naked through the narrow hall

startling the girl who was climbing down the ladder from her loft—

she crouched, her eyes wide.

I seemed to see us both like that—the naked walking woman,

the crouching girl—two animals in the world.

You scared me, she said.

And you scared me, I said,

from the bathroom—already looking for makeup and cream.

The Teacher

Was he my husband, my lover, my teacher?

One book will say one thing. Another book another.

Can the body love beyond hunger?

You tell me what you know of desire and surrender.

I had a teacher who would not hurt me. I had a teacher

who struck me in the face, then struck me again.

I had a teacher who died in his own bed, a teacher who

died in public, a teacher who was a child, a girl.

Can we love without greed? Without wanting to be first?

Everyone wanted to pour his wine, to sit near him at the table.

Me too. Until he was dead.

Then he was with me all the time.

Fourteen

She is still mine—for another year or so,

but she is already looking past me

through the funeral-home door

to where the boys have gathered in their dark suits.

Adaptation

Last night, cleaning the counters after dinner, the girl said,

Would you want to know the date of your death?

No, I said, I would not want to know that.

I would, she said.

Then she said, If someone killed you

would you want to come back for revenge?

No, I said, I'd rather come back to the people I loved.

What if you came back to someone and they'd forgotten you? she said.

I'd tell them I loved them anyway, I said,

What if they said *Who*?

I scrubbed the pans for a while.

That night we decided to watch something other than the murder mysteries

we'd been watching for months

and chose an Edith Wharton adaptation,

wealthy young American girls flocking to England to acquire husbands

—every single one of them chose the wrong man.

Why do they all do that? I said from the couch;

and from the pink chair she said, Mom there wouldn't be any story

if they all chose well.

By the time the first episode was over we were in darkness,

both of us, wrapped in blankets shouting No no no no

when the last most vibrant girl agreed to marry the rich sop.

The credits rolled. 17 seconds to the next episode. 16, 15, 14,

Another one? she said.

Sure, I said, looking at the clock.   And she clicked.

October

The first cold morning, the little pumpkins lined up at the corner market, and

the girl walks along Hudson Street to school and doesn't look back.

The old sorrow blows in with the scent of wood smoke

as I walk up the five flights to our apartment and lean hard against

the broken dishwasher so it will run. Then it comes to me: Yes I'll die,

so will everyone, so *has* everyone. It's what we have in common.

And, for a moment, the sorrow ceased, and I saw that it hadn't been sorrow

after all, but loneliness, and for a few moments, it was gone.

Delivery

The delivery man slowly climbs

the five steep flights of stairs

as I lean down to watch him walking up

as he's talking on the phone

and now he pauses

on the third floor landing

to touch a little Christmas light

the girl had wrapped around the banister—

speaking to someone in a language

so melodic I ask him what—

when he hands the package to me,

and he says Patois—from Jamaica—

smiling up at me from where he's standing

on the landing

a smile so radiant that

re-entering the apartment I'm

a young woman again, and

the sweetness of the men I've loved walks in,

through the closed door

one of them right now,

kicking the snow off his boots,

turning to take my face in his cold hands,

kissing me now with his cold mouth.

Magdalene at the Theopoetics Conference

Yes, the scholar said, but why ask your students

to write these close observations?

What use is it to notice the rusted drainpipe?

The young woman asleep in the library

her head resting on her folded arms?

Why should they look inside the petals of the pink tulip

to the yellow pollen-coated stamen?

Or under their beds to where the dust has collected?

Don't you want them to seek the divine?

One Day

One day the patterned carpet, the folding chairs,

the woman in the blue suit by the door examining her split ends,

all of it will go on without me. I'll have disappeared,

as easily as a coin under lake water, and few to notice the difference

—a coin dropping into the darkening—

and West 4th Street, the sesame noodles that taste like

too much peanut butter lowered into the small white paper carton

—all of it will go on and on

and the I that caused me so much trouble? Nowhere

or grit thrown into the garden

or into the sticky bodies of several worms,

or just gone, stopped—like the Middle Ages,

like the coin Whitman carried in his pocket all the way to that basement bar on Broadway that isn't there anymore.

Oh to be in Whitman's pocket, on a cold winter day,

to feel his large warm hand slide in and out, and in again.

To be taken hold of by Walt Whitman! To be exchanged!

To be spent for something somebody wanted and drank and found delicious.

Magdalene Afterwards

Remember the woman in the blue burka forced to kneel in the stadium

then shot in the head?   That was me.

And I was the woman who secretly filmed it.

I was burned as a witch by the people in my own town

I was sent to the asylum at 16.

I was walking with my younger sister, looking for firewood,

when we saw the group of men approaching.

I'm the woman so in love with my husband

sometimes I wait in the kitchen chair and stare at the door.

I'm bored at the business meeting,

impatient with the Do Not Walk sign.

I'm parked in my wheelchair with the others in the hallway

—three hours till lunch, I don't remember who it is

who leans down to kiss me.

I've forgotten my keys, dropped the dish, fallen down

the icy stoop.

I'm sitting on the bench with my bags, waiting for the bus.

I'm the woman in the black suit hailing a taxi.

I'm in prayer, in meditation, I've shaved my head, I wear robes

now instead of dresses.

I've entered the classroom and all the children call out my name at once.

I'm talking on my cell phone while driving.

I'm walking the goats out to the far field, gazing at the mountain

I've looked at every day of my life.

I never had children,

I bore nine living children and two dead ones

I adopted a girl in my late middle age

I'm cooking rice and beans

cooking dal

cooking lamb

reheating pizza

lighting the candles on the birthday cake

standing quietly by the window

still hungry for I don't know what.

I want to see through the red bricks of the building across the street,

into the something else that almost gleams through the day.

Often, I'm lonely.

Sometimes a joy pours through me so immense.

ACKNOWLEDGMENTS

With gratitude and in memory of dear companions: Lucie Brock-Broido, Tony Hoagland, Richard McCann, and Jason Shinder.

Thank you to beloved, brilliant friends (members of our writing group) who critiqued and encouraged many of the new poems: Sophie Cabot Black, Mark Conway, Vie Vee Francis, Ricky Gordon, Michael Klein, Nick Flynn, Donna Masini, and Victoria Redel.

Thank you to my beloved Grace Yi-nan Howe, for your clear gaze, fearless editing, and empowering love.

Thank you to the amazing Maria Popova for The Universe in Verse which engendered The Singularity.

Thank you to Jim Moore, beloved poetry sponsor, for your presence and your poems.

Thank you to the indefatigable Bill Clegg for saying, Yes, that's a good idea.

Thank you to Jill Bialosky for bringing me home to W. W. Norton, for the years of our collaboration, for your insights, encouragement, and care.

Thank you to Drew Weitman and all the people at W. W. Norton for your gracious and patient attention.

Thank you to Persea Books, publisher of The Good Thief in 1988, still in print and on sale today.

Thank you to the editors of The New Yorker, POETRY, Ploughshares, and The Marginalian, where some of the new poems appeared.

INDEX OF TITLES AND FIRST LINES